One Morning in Joseph's Garden

An Easter Story

Barbara Younger and Lisa Flinn

Illustrated by Joe Boddy

ABINGDON PRESS

Nashville

ONE MORNING IN JOSEPH'S GARDEN

Copyright © 1998 by Abingdon Press

ISBN 0-687-09550-6

To Bill and Cliff, who help tend God's garden

98 99 00 01 02 03 04 05 06 07 — 10 9 8 7 6 5 4 3 2 1

PRINTED IN HONG KONG

A brilliant light shone in Joseph's garden, yet the morning had not come. The brightness surrounded a tomb cut into the rock wall of the garden where Jesus had been buried.

The oak tree stood solemn as the light sent rays through its branches.

In the cedar, a nest of sparrows awoke and broke the silence with a song.

The leaves of the weeping willow glistened.
The ancient olive tree had seen many dawns,
but somehow this was different.

A lizard appeared from a crack to investigate.

Ants, anxious to begin the day's activities, sent out scouts from their underground home.

The light filtered through the walls of the beehive and rallied the workers to action.

Doves perched on a thorn tree and watched with interest. Somehow they sensed that this moment was important.

Lilies, irises, and poppies
turned to face
the light.

A snake, feeling a bit uneasy, slithered away.
Startled, a frog leapt into the water trough.

Two rabbits, who were nibbling dandelion greens, looked up.

The stone covering the tomb moved.
Footsteps touched the soil.

Darkness returned to Joseph's garden.

Hours later, the gate creaked. A woman came into the garden and looked into the tomb.

She left on hurried feet and returned with two men.

After a time the garden was still, except for the sound of the woman crying.

The darkness over all Jerusalem began to fade as dawn stretched through the clouds.

The woman, who was standing amid herbs of mint and hyssop, said, "They have taken away my Lord."

Turning from the tomb, she saw the gardener.
"Sir, if you have carried him away, tell me where you have laid him."

The gardener said to her, "Mary."
Then Mary knew.
The gardener was
Jesus. He had risen
from the dead.

That morning in Joseph's garden the flowers, the herbs, the trees, and all of the creatures were witness to the Resurrection.

And what a morning that was!

A Word to Adults

Before we wrote this story, we read about the gardens of the Holy Land.

We learned that people in Bible days grew trees, fruits, vegetables, herbs, and flowers together in their gardens. Stone troughs were used to send water from nearby streams to the garden's thirsty plants. People went to their gardens to gather food or to enjoy quiet time. Of course birds, bugs, and other creatures lived in the garden or went there for food or rest.

Gardens were also used as burial places. Joseph of Arimathea was a wealthy man who had a brand new tomb in his garden. After Jesus' body was taken down from the cross, Joseph allowed the body to be placed in that tomb.

In the years since the resurrection of Jesus, Christians have given symbolic meaning to many of the features of the natural world. Listed below are the meanings of the natural symbols used in our story.

LIGHT:	The coming of Jesus	LILY:	Purity, Resurrection, Mary, the mother of Jesus
ROCK:	God or Jesus		
CEDAR:	The everlasting Kingdom of God, or God's everlasting love for God's children	IRIS:	The Holy Trinity, Mary, the mother of Jesus
		POPPY:	Sleep or death
OAK:	Jesus	SNAKE:	Evil or our sinfulness
SPARROW:	A lowly person	FROG:	Worldly things
WILLOW:	The gospel of Jesus	WATER:	Baptism
OLIVE:	Peace	RABBIT:	Hope in Christ, new life
LIZARD:	The soul that seeks God	DANDELION:	The bitter herbs of Passover
BEEHIVE:	The church	FEET:	Willing servitude
BEE:	The hard-working Christian	GATE:	Jesus
DOVE:	The Holy Spirit	CLOUDS:	The unseen God
THORN:	Grief	MINT:	God's healing power
		HYSSOP:	Humility